Tact and Finesse

Communicating with Challenging Personalities

Table of Contents

Chapter 1. Introduction

Navigating complex conversations is more of an art than a science, yet it is a skill that everyone can learn to master. Our Special Report titled "Tact and Finesse: Communicating with Challenging Personalities" takes you on the fascinating journey of perfecting your communication game. Imagine being able to transform even the most difficult interactions into productive and positive engagements! We'll show you how to not only weather the stormy seas of challenging personalities, but also to guide your communication ship confidently to the harbour of mutual understanding and respect. Embellished with real-world examples, expert insights, and practical strategies, this report is a must-have toolkit for anyone aspiring to become more effective in their personal and professional interactions. Guaranteed, you'll end up eagerly sharing your newly found communication treasures with everyone! So are you ready to sail these uncharted waters of tactful communication?

Chapter 2. Understanding Challenging Personalities

Challenging personalities can pose a significant obstacle in any communicative setting, especially in the workplace or personal relationships. These individuals may have behavioral patterns that can sometimes be hard to decipher or deal with. This chapter aims to help us understand these personalities, their underlying motives, and how we can adapt our communication approach to create a more harmonious and efficient interaction environment.

2.1. Understanding Behavioral Patterns

The first step in dealing with challenging personalities is understanding their behavioral patterns. Some individuals may have behaviors that are continuously problematic. Others may present challenges only in certain situations or interactions. Identifying consistent traits and patterns can provide valuable insights into how these individuals perceive the world and how they may respond to various communication approaches.

For instance, someone who often interrupts or talks over others might be expressing a need to be heard or understood. Conversely, a person who is consistently quiet or withdrawn might be experiencing discomfort in social situations or might struggle with self-expression.

Curiously observing these behaviors, preferably without judgment or assumptions, can offer a starting point for determining the most effective tactics for communication. Once we better understand these patterns, we can tailor our approach to accommodate their style and meet them where they are.

2.2. The Role of Emotional Intelligence

Greater self-awareness and an understanding of emotional intelligence (EI) can significantly improve our ability to navigate difficult conversations. Emotional intelligence, as psychologist and author Daniel Goleman explains, involves understanding our own emotions and those of others.

Through emotional intelligence, we can better manage our reactions, empathize with others, and guide our communications to reach a positive outcome. When dealing with challenging personalities, having a high degree of emotional intelligence can allow us to appropriately address the emotional needs of others whilst maintaining our own emotional wellbeing.

By understanding the motivations and emotions behind various behaviors, we can develop a more nuanced understanding of how to engage effectively with complex personalities. Emotional intelligence can provide us with the tools we need to approach these situations thoughtfully and empathetically.

2.3. Personality Types and Communication Styles

Understanding different personality types and their inherent communication styles can also be an effective strategy when dealing with challenging personalities. Psychologists have identified numerous personality types, each with its unique set of characteristics, strengths, and weaknesses.

Based on Swiss psychiatrist Carl Jung's theory, the Myers-Briggs Type Indicator (MBTI) is a popular framework in contemporary psychology, identifying 16 personality types. Each type is associated with specific preferences for information processing and decision-making, which in turn, influence their communication style.

It's important to remember that our aim should be to appreciate and respond to these individual differences rather than trying to change the other person's communication style. By aligning our communication strategies to their specific style, we can enhance our interaction effectiveness.

2.4. Adjusting Your Communication Approach

Having identified the behavioural patterns and understood the communication style of the challenging personality, the next step involves adapting our own communication approach. Each conversation can be viewed as a shared journey, which requires both parties to navigate sometimes difficult terrain to reach a mutual understanding.

Knowing when to be assertive and when to be yielding, when to ask questions and when to listen, when to push for a decision, and when to give space for contemplation – these are the nuanced skills that define an effective communicator. A more mindful, patient, and empathetic communication strategy can help establish common ground and promote understanding.

Everyone's communication style is unique and dynamic, continuously evolving depending on various factors such as mental state, the context of interaction, and the individual's personality type. By recognizing this and adjusting our approach accordingly, we can chart a course that best arrives at the desired destination: understanding and respect.

2.5. The Power of Reflective Listening

Listening transcends hearing; it's about understanding and interpreting the messages others are conveying. Reflective listening, a vital tool in our communication arsenal, involves echoing back a person's statement to show them that you've understood exactly what they meant.

Use this technique to show empathy, validate their feelings, and encourage further conversation. Reflective listening can be especially effective when dealing with challenging personalities, as it shows our earnest willingness to understand their perspective.

Consequently, when we focus on listening and reflecting rather than asserting our view, we create a space for open dialogue, making those with even the most challenging personalities feel heard and respected. This leads to the engagement of more productive and positive interactions.

Mastering the art of communicating with challenging personalities is all about awareness, empathy, and flexibility. By following these strategies, we can turn the tide on difficult interactions and chart a course towards effective and harmonious discourse. Remember, everyone we meet can teach us something valuable, and every conversation is a new opportunity for growth and understanding.

Chapter 3. Navigating Difficult Conversations With Ease

Starting a difficult, high-stakes conversation is a challenge that we all face, whether it's at home, at work, or in any other social context. The ability to deal effectively with these types of discussions is crucial.

3.1. Understanding Difficult Conversations

Understanding why a conversation is difficult can often help in navigating them. Difficult conversations tend to derive from disagreements, conflicts, misunderstandings, or differing perspectives. It might be about differing objectives at work, variation in philosophies of life, contrasting values or beliefs, or any other topic that can be a source of disagreement. Understanding the root of the discussion can guide your navigation.

3.2. Preparations: Laying the Groundwork

Before you even begin the discussion, there are a few steps you need to take. First off, getting into the proper frame of mind is essential. You should take a few moments to calm your mind and to put aside any bias or emotions related to the conversation.

Next, put yourself in the other person's shoes. Attempt to understand their perspective, the reasons why they hold their view, and potential hidden emotions or anxieties. Acknowledging these issues upfront can help your conversation flow more smoothly.

By having a clear idea of your objectives for the conversation, and your best alternatives if agreement cannot be reached, you can help align your actions with your goals.

3.3. The Art of Listening

Listening is one of the most overlooked skills during critical conversations. We sometimes tend to focus on framing our responses while the other person is still talking. By fully listening, we show respect and make the other person feel heard, understood, and validated. It opens up the door for them to do the same for you.

3.4. Constructive Feedback: A Two-Way Street

Feedback is an essential part of any conversation. Giving constructive feedback helps inform the other person about viewpoints they may have missed while receiving feedback allows for more understanding and improves the conversation.

Such feedback should be specific, noting particular instances or examples rather than making generalizations. It should also be helpful and contribute positively to the discussion. Pay attention to your language: using 'I' statements, as opposed to 'you' statements, helps reduce defensiveness.

3.5. Bridging the Divide: Finding Common Ground

The best way to handle a difficult conversation is to turn adversaries into collaborators, working together towards a common goal. Find shared interests, experiences, or values that you can connect on. This is often a good starting point for a more constructive conversation.

3.6. The Role of Body Language

Humans communicate not only through words but also through their body language. Positive nonverbal cues like maintaining eye contact, having an open posture, and nodding attentively can make the other person feel heard and appreciated.

In a difficult conversation, these cues can be used to give reassurances, show empathy, and convey sincerity. However, be cautious about negative body language: crossing arms, avoiding eye contact, or checking the time can send signals of disinterest, hostility, or impatience.

3.7. Ending Conversations Constructively

If the conversation becomes too heated, it might be best to take a break and revisit the topic when both parties have cooled down. Always remember your objectives and that the aim is to improve understanding, not necessarily to change the other person's view.

End on a positive note, doing your best to acknowledge the other person's viewpoint and emphasizing the importance of the relationship. Even if agreement wasn't reached, expressing appreciation for being open to the discussion establishes a base for future conservations.

By understanding, preparing, listening, offering constructive feedback, bridging the gap, being aware of your body language, and ending constructively, you can navigate difficult conversations with finesse. Like any skill, these strategies require practice, but they lead to better communication, greater understanding, and stronger relationships. You'll start seeing difficult discussions less like obstacles, and more like opportunities to grow. So be ready, explore the art of tactful conversation, and voyage into a world of meaningful and respectful communication.

Chapter 4. Mastering the Art of Active Listening

Active listening, a fundamental skill in human communication, is where the listener gives their full attention to the speaker. Instead of passively receiving information, the listener is involved, internalizing and comprehending the content. It is a vital tool for clear and effective communication, greatly enhancing our interactions with challenging personalities.

4.1. Understanding Active Listening

Active listening encompasses more than merely hearing the spoken words. It involves understanding the message being conveyed and showing interest by providing feedback. As an active participant in the conversation, you are required to understand, respond, and recall the discussion.

For active listening to happen effectively, one must practice patience to let the speaker convey their thoughts without interruption. This aspect is particularly useful in situations where the speaker possesses a challenging personality where interruptions can derail communication leading to misunderstanding or conflict.

4.2. The Fundamentals of Active Listening

Attending to verbal and non-verbal cues forms the basis of active listening. Verbal cues include tone and pace, suspensions, and emphasis on particular words. Non-verbal cues like facial expressions, body language, and gestures often convey feelings and attitudes which spoken words might miss.

Now, let's explore the key elements of active listening:

1. Providing undivided attention
2. Show understanding
3. Providing feedback
4. Defer judgement
5. Responding appropriately

4.3. Providing Undivided Attention

Cultivating concentration and mindfulness is the first step to providing undivided attention. In this era of digital distractions, maintaining focus on a conversation may prove challenging. Turn off your devices or put them away and respect the speaker's space by being fully present.

Non-verbal cues such as maintaining direct eye contact, nodding at appropriate intervals, and adopting an open body posture demonstrate your commitment and eagerness to the speaker. Even when on a phone conversation where the speaker cannot see you, simple verbal affirmations like 'yes', 'uh-huh', and 'I see' can assure them of your full attention.

4.4. Show Understanding

Active listening aims not only to listen but to also comprehend and retain the information conveyed. This is accomplished by paraphrasing or rephrasing the speaker's words. It ensures you have grasped their ideas and allows confirmation or clarification if there were misunderstandings. Try to keep your rephrase succinct but thorough and avoid offering advice or critique at this juncture unless explicitly asked.

4.5. Providing Feedback

Feedback allows for interactions and discussions. It exhibits empathy towards the speaker. Start with phrases like 'It sounds like', 'So you feel that', etc., when offering feedback to avoid sounding judgmental or confrontational. Revolving the conversation around the speaker's sentiments instead of your perception enables them to open up and freely communicate their thoughts and feelings.

4.6. Defer Judgement

Holding off judgement until the speaker is finished is fundamental to active listening. Quick conclusions based on half information can cloud your understanding, leading to skewed responses and potentially aggrieving the speaker. Reserve your opinions, disagreements or rebuttals for after they have conveyed their entire message.

4.7. Responding Appropriately

Being respectful in your responses is critical. This is particularly significant in conversations with challenging individuals where inappropriate responses can escalate conflicts. Keep your language professional and your emotions in check, even when countering their views.

4.8. The Power of Silence

Silence, at the right moments, can play a pivotal role in active listening. It allows for reflection, enabling both the listener and the speaker to digest and process the information. Managed effectively, silence offers space for the speaker to either confirm your understanding or furnish more detail. However, beware of prolonged silence as it might project disinterest or discomfort and ultimately mar the conversation.

Active listening is not necessarily instinctive and requires conscious practice. Developing these skills will not only make you a better listener but also a more effective communicator, capable of navigating challenging personalities with tact and finesse. By remaining dedicated, you'll find your conversational prowess becoming increasingly refined, leading to productive and positive engagements. It's a journey akin to sailing through uncharted waters, with the reward being a treasure trove of enhanced personal and professional relationships.

Chapter 5. The Power of Empathy in Difficult Communications

Human interaction is a dynamic and multidimensional process, with empathy playing a critical role, particularly in challenging conversations. Often, the most challenging personalities can be reached with a powerful tool: empathy. Understanding their emotions and motivations can help reduce conflict and facilitate resolution.

5.1. The Essence of Empathy

Empathy, quite simply, is the ability to understand and share the feelings of others. To feel empathy does not necessitate agreement; rather, it's about comprehension and perspective-taking, which fosters connection and builds trust with another person. But why is empathy so crucial when dealing with challenging personalities?

Challenging personalities often act the way they do because of underlying insecurities or frustrations. Empathy allows us to see beyond surface-level behaviours and understand these root causes. This understanding then enables us to respond in a way that tailors our approach to their unique personality and situation, transforming a potentially confrontational interaction into a more constructive one.

5.2. Empathy Vs Sympathy

Before unpacking how to harness empathy, it's important to distinguish empathy from sympathy. Sympathy implies feelings of pity or sorrow for someone else's misfortune. It's a feeling of compassion, but from a distance. Empathy, however, involves experiencing another person's emotions as if they were your own. This intrinsic understanding is what allows a true, genuine connection: it is not about looking down on their situation, but feeling with them.

5.3. The Role of Active Listening

Key to empathetic communication is active listening. This process includes giving the speaker your undivided attention, withholding judgement, reflecting, clarifying, summarizing, and sharing. By doing so, it allows full comprehension of the speaker's experience and feelings.

Active listening affords the opportunity to spot nuances and unspoken sentiments that precisely project the speaker's emotions. Commenting on these observations can help validate their feelings and show them that you understand.

5.4. Emotional Intelligence and Empathy

Emotional Intelligence (EQ) is the ability to recognize, understand, and manage our own emotions and the emotions of others. A key component of EQ is empathy. When engaged in a difficult conversation, understanding your emotions as well as the other's person allows for a more controlled, thoughtful response. EQ provides a framework for communicating empathetically, recognizing when to ask for clarification, and when to steer the conversation in a more positive direction.

5.5. Practical Empathy-Building Strategies

Here are some practical strategies to help cultivate empathy in our conversations:

1. **Ask Insightful Questions:** Rather than making assumptions, ask questions to try and gain a deeper understanding of the other person's feelings, perspectives, or motivations.

2. **Use Nonjudgmental Responses:** Avoid replaying with judgment or criticism.

3. **Be Fully Present:** Try to be present in the moment, putting aside any distractions or preoccupations.

4. **Encourage:** Provide encouragements or affirmations. Let them know you're listening and don't underestimate the power of well-timed reassurances.

5. **Reflect Feelings:** Sometimes, repeating back to the speaker what you understand their feelings to be can help confirm that you have understood correctly. It also shows that you are taking their feelings seriously.

6. **Validate:** Occasionally, offer some form of validation that their feelings are understandable given their situation.

5.6. Empathy in Action

Consider, for instance, a notoriously short-tempered colleague who frequently snaps during meetings. Before allowing this to frustrate you or escalate into conflict, try empathizing instead. Understand that their behaviour may be the result of stress, an intense workload, or personal issues. This doesn't excuse ill behaviour, but it gives reason to it, granting you enough patience and understanding to deal with it more tactfully. In conversation with them, express your understanding, validating their stress without condoning their behaviour, opening avenues for effective discussions around it.

5.7. The Golden Rule of Empathy

The principle of treating others as you would want to be treated not only advances harmonious interaction but also promotes deeply empathic exchanges rooted in mutual respect and understanding. Ultimately, employing empathy increases your ability to influence, motivate, and connect with people, turning difficult conversations into opportunities for growth.

By honing these empathy skills and integrating them into your conversations, you can change the trajectory of problematic interactions. This shift has the power to transform challenging personalities into unique opportunities for growth, understanding, and even camaraderie.

Chapter 6. Strategic Use of Questions for Better Interactions

One of the most potent tools in communication is the art of probing, the skill of asking questions. This section explores the strategic use of questions to navigate and manage challenging interactions while building rapport and empathy along the way.

6.1. The Purpose of Questions

Questions are more than mere tools to seek information. They serve myriad functions, and their strategic use can be transformative.

Firstly, questions engage and involve the other person. They make your conversation partner feel heard and valued. Secondly, questions give us control of the conversation, allowing us to guide its direction and pace effectively, especially in difficult situations.

Moreover, questions give us the chance to understand others' perspectives. We learn more about their thoughts, feelings, and motivations. Finally, well-planned questions can disarm hostility, diffuse tension and mitigate confrontational scenarios, all the while promoting rapport and respect.

6.2. Mastering the Act of Probing

To wield the power of questions effectively, we need to understand the types and timing of questions, as well as techniques to encourage answers.

There are two primary types of probing: Open and Closed questions.

Open inquiries encourage broad, expansive answers. They elicit ideas, narratives and feelings. For example, 'How did you feel about the meeting?' promotes longer conversation than the closed version 'Did you enjoy the meeting?'.

Closed questions, on the other hand, limit answers to brief or single-word responses, often a 'yes' or 'no'. They provide specific information and are particularly useful when you need clarity or have to control the conversation's length.

The timing of your questions can also impact their effectiveness. Positively phrased questions asked at the right moment can reduce defensiveness and increase openness. Asking 'What can we do to improve?' at the end of a critique can serve to focus on solutions, rather than dwelling on problems.

To encourage answers, cultivate a comfortable environment where the person feels safe to express their thoughts. Patiently wait for the response without interrupting, and acknowledge statements with empathy.

6.3. Defusing with the Right Questions

A challenging interaction often arrives with a thorny bundle of emotions. The right questions can act as a defusing agent, dispelling tension and helping recenter the conversation.

Ask about feelings: 'Can you tell me more about how you're feeling?' This can allow ventilation of suppressed emotions, normalizing and calming the situation.

Redirect towards solutions: 'What do you think we could do to make things better?' This shifts focus away from the problem and toward solutions, aiding conflict resolution.

Validating questions reassert the individual's worth: 'It seems like you've put a lot of thought into this, haven't you?' It reinforces their value and promotes constructive conversation.

6.4. Reflective Questions: Mirrors to The Soul

Reflective questions hold a mirror to the individual's reactions and feelings, promoting self-awareness and introspection. 'What does that tell you about how you reacted?' encourages examination of personal emotions and reactions. This technique can be healing and transformative, particularly in managing difficult interactions.

6.5. Using Questions for Persuasion

Questions are also persuasive tools. We can steer a person towards revealing their needs, aligning with our goals, or gaining new insights through strategic questioning.

Confirmation questions reinforce agreement: 'So, you agree that this is the best approach?'

Implication questions reveal consequences: 'What do you think would happen if we don't solve this issue?'

Hypothetical questions explore alternatives: 'How would you approach this if you were in my position?'

Neutrally presented, these inquiries can influence opinions subtly and enhance mutual understanding.

6.6. Questions as a Learning Tool

Finally, use questions as a tool to facilitate learning. Through effective questioning, we can foster deep thinking, exploration of ideas, reflection, and growth in the other person. It constructs a platform for development and understanding, empowering individuals in the process.

Mastering the art of questioning takes practice, but the rewards are well worth the effort. When used strategically, questions can turn a challenging interaction into a fruitful one, fostering respect, mutual understanding and, eventually, success in communication. It is akin to having your own navigation compass in the uncharted waters of complicated interactions.

Chapter 7. Non-verbal Communication: Reading Between the Lines

Communication doesn't always have to happen with words. In fact, a significant part of our daily communication is non-verbal. Non-verbal cues, if deciphered correctly, can give you deep insights into a person's feelings, emotions, and intentions. Mastering the art of reading these non-verbal cues can transform your interpersonal communication skills and open you up to a new level of understanding and empathy.

7.1. The Power of Non-Verbal Communication

Often, it is not the words, but how we say them that matters. Non-verbal communication involves how we speak, gestures, body language, facial expressions, and even silence. It's as integral in communication as words, sometimes even more. When words fail, or when they contradict non-verbal cues, people tend to rely more on the non-verbal elements of the conversation. Deception, anxiety, hatred, love – all these emotions can be effectively showcased or concealed using non-verbal cues.

Understanding the importance of non-verbal communication will help you to perceive what isn't being said out loud and thus enrich your communication skills.

7.2. Decoding Body Language

Body language is the unspoken element of communication that we use to reveal our true feelings and thoughts, whether consciously or unconsciously. It includes body movements and gestures (positive, negative, neutral), posture, eye contact and how these sync with verbal communication.

Let's delve deeper into some aspects of body language:

1. **Posture:** An erect posture suggests confidence and high self-esteem, while a slouched posture may suggest the opposite.

2. **Arm Cross:** A person crossing their arms might be showing defensiveness or resistance.

3. **Eye Contact:** Sufficient eye contact shows interest and engagement, while too much or too little might make the other person uncomfortable.

Effective communication demands awareness of these subtle body language cues in order to truly understand others and adjust our posture and gestures accordingly.

7.3. Facial Expressions and Their Interpretations

Face is the window to the soul goes the saying, and rightly so. From happiness to sorrow, from anger to surprise, facial expressions can reflect a wide range of emotions. Some facial expressions are universal, like a smile indicating happiness or pleasure and a frown showing unhappiness or displeasure.

However, like any other non-verbal communication tool, facial expressions too can be tricky sometimes. For instance, a smile might not always signify happiness; it may even be a mask to hide embarrassment or discomfort. Similarly, a frowned face might not necessarily mean displeasure; it could also mean deep contemplation.

Thus, while reading facial expressions, one must also consider the context, culture, and individual personality facets.

7.4. Proxemics: The Art of Using Space

Non-verbal communication is not just about reading the signs given by people; it's also about understanding the space between individuals while they interact, known as proxemics. There are broadly four types of spaces:

1. **Intimate Space:** This is typically reserved for close connections, like friends and family.

2. **Personal Space:** This is space around someone in which others can't come without feeling uncomfortable unless they are exceptionally close to the person.

3. **Social Space:** This space is for interactions among acquaintances.

4. **Public Space:** This is the space where anyone can interact with others without breaching personal boundaries.

Understanding these zones and their significance can drastically improve your communication skills, making you more effective and empathic in your interactions.

7.5. Paralinguistics: It's Not What You Say, It's How You Say It

Paralinguistics refer to vocal communication that isn't actual words - tone, pitch, loudness, inflection, and speed. You might be saying the most positive words, but if your tone is negative, that's what people will remember. Paralinguistics often express emotions, influence interpretations, and set the tone of the conversation. For instance, a high pitched, fast-paced voice might indicate excitement or nervousness, while a low, slow speech might suggest sadness or exhaustion.

7.6. Deciphering Silence: The Language of the Unsaid

Silence, often overlooked, is a powerful tool in the non-verbal communication toolbox. Its significance varies widely based on the context. Silence can signify thoughtfulness, discomfort, tensions, agreement, or anger. It's crucial to decipher this powerful yet ambiguous tool, as misinterpretation can lead to misunderstanding and conflict.

7.7. Reflecting and Responding: The Roots of Mutual Understanding

Reading non-verbal cues is only half the task; responding effectively is equally important. It's crucial to reflect on the cues picked up, be sensitive, and then respond in a way that enhances mutual understanding and respect. For instance, if you find someone's arms crossed and a frown on their face, it's better to ease the situation rather than adding fuel to the fire.

In conclusion, mastering non-verbal communication involves being aware, observant, empathetic, and responsive. It's an art that, when mastered, can transform your ability to navigate through personal and professional relationships. Instead of just hearing words, you'll be able to comprehend emotions and thoughts - reading between the lines, translating the language of the unsaid, and communicating with more finesse and tact. Embarking on this journey of understanding and empathizing is indeed a rewarding voyage into the uncharted waters of human interactions.

Chapter 8. Tactful Feedback: Giving and Receiving Criticism

A critical part of any productive and meaningful dialogue is feedback. However, providing and accepting feedback can be a challenging task. It requires the delicate balance of honesty and respect, giving and receiving criticism in a constructive and beneficial manner. This chapter will guide you through the nuances of delivering and accepting criticism through tactful communication.

8.1. Understanding the Importance of Feedback in Communication

Feedback is an essential tool in any communication. It helps to confirm that a message has been correctly interpreted and serves as a platform for the development and improvement of relationships and performance. Whether it's a work scenario where you're giving your team feedback or a personal relationship where you're responding to a friend's actions, the way this criticism is communicated can have significant implications.

Criticism, delivered and received properly, can be a powerful tool for growth. Considering this, the true art in criticism lies not merely within the process of pointing out faults or praise, but in the manner in which these observations are communicated and reacted to.

8.2. Constructive versus Destructive Criticism

Before we dive into the art of giving and receiving criticism tactfully, let's differentiate between constructive and destructive criticism. Constructive criticism, as its name suggests, is meant to construct, build, or improve something. It focuses on specific behaviours or actions that need to be changed and equips the recipient with solutions or suggestions for improvement.

On the other hand, destructive criticism tends to be negative, focusing on a person's weaknesses with the intent to harm, belittle, or mock. This type of feedback often lacks specific, actionable insights for improvement and typically leaves the recipient feeling defeated or insulted.

Understanding the difference between these two types can make the process of providing and responding to feedback more effective and beneficial.

8.3. The Art of Delivering Tactful Feedback

Giving feedback or criticism requires tact and sensitivity. Here are some suggestions on how to deliver feedback that will be taken as constructive:

1. Be Specific: Base your feedback on observable behavior rather than on personal traits.

2. Be Timely: Give feedback as soon as possible after the event, while it's still fresh in everyone's mind.

3. Use "I" Statements: This allows you to express how you feel about the situation and makes it easier for the recipient to accept your viewpoint without feeling attacked.

4. End on a Positive Note: This technique does not diminish the importance of the feedback but stresses that despite the criticism, you value the individual and have confidence in their ability to improve.

5. Suggest Actionable Steps: Provide recommendations for improvement—they can act as roadmaps for the receiver to act upon the feedback.

8.4. The Grace of Accepting Feedback

Accepting criticism, whether constructive or destructive, can be challenging. However, receiving feedback gracefully is as crucial as providing it. Here are some pointers to handling criticism:

1. Stay Calm: Treat the feedback as an opportunity to learn and grow. Suppressing negative emotions will help you to think more clearly and respond more constructively.

2. Seek Clarification: If any point is unclear or you feel the feedback is baseless, respectfully ask for clarification.

3. Reframe Criticism: Reframing the received criticism as an avenue for growth can transform a negative experience into a productive one.

4. Show Gratitude: Even if the criticism is difficult to accept, express gratitude to the feedback giver. This appreciation reflects your maturity and willingness to learn.

5. Reflect and Act: Post-feedback, take some time to review the information, decide on its validity and act on areas for improvement.

8.5. The Double-Edged Sword of Feedback

Feedback, though often seen as exclusively corrective, can also be a form of appreciation. Be generous with positive feedback. It plays an equally important role in communication, fostering motivation, and encouraging the repetition of good practices or behaviours.

However, avoid 'sandwiching' criticism between two complements. This can confuse the receiver about the feedback's intention and undermine the importance of the proposed improvements.

Balancing feedback between appreciation and criticism is a learned skill. The goal is to create an environment where both praise and constructive criticism drive growth and improvement.

8.6. The Continuing Journey of Tactful Feedback

Mastering the art of tactful feedback—both giving and receiving—is a continuous journey. It requires practice, patience, and humility. Mistakes will be made and lessons will be learned but with time and experience, this skill can be honed to perfection. The overall goal is to foster positive and productive communication environments, whether in our personal or professional lives.

In a world where communication is often rushed and can appear insensitive, the art of providing tactful feedback requires us to slow down, think about our words, their interpretation, and the effects they may have.

As we hone the use of tactful feedback in our communication arsenal, we also develop empathy, understanding, and respect towards our social and professional circle. This growth is a boon not just for our individual selves, but also for those we interact with – truly crafting a mutually benefitting communication environment.

This chapter concludes here, but the journey of effective communication continues. You are now equipped with valuable strategies to successfully navigate the rough seas of criticism, helping you to work towards comprehensive and compassionate communication. Indeed, mastering the art of tactful feedback is a leap forward in your voyage of achieving effective communication.

Chapter 9. Adapting to Communication Styles: The Versatility Key

Versatility in communication is akin to a chameleon changing its colours, adapting itself to the environment. It demands a deep understanding of varying communication styles and an ability to adjust one's own style accordingly, making this the key to effectively deal with different personalities. Let's delve into the panorama of communication styles and how to master this art.

9.1. Understanding Different Communication Styles

There are four primary communication styles: the Director, the Expressive, the Thinker, and the Supportive. Each comes with its unique set of strengths and potential areas of improvement.

The Director is assertive and to-the-point. They thrive on action and results. With an analytical approach, their ideal environment is where decision-making is prompt and logical. The challenge with Directors, sometimes, can be their inability to empathize and be patient.

The Expressive is outgoing and enthusiastic, often making a lasting impression. They can inspire others by their charm and magnetic charisma but might be prone to emotional outbursts and may lack focus.

The Thinker is organized, detail-oriented, and logical. They appreciate accuracy and a systematic approach. However, their tendency to over-analyze can lead to procrastination or make them appear uncaring.

The Supportive is a good listener, team player, friendly, and focused on relationships. They may however struggle with assertiveness and resist change.

It's important to note that while people may primarily demonstrate one style, they usually have elements of the others too, and swap their styles according to different situations.

9.2. Assessing Your Own Style

After understanding these styles, it's time to reflect and identify your own primary communication style. Self-awareness is the foundation on which you can build upon your adaptation strategies. Acknowledge your strengths and understand that the less desirable traits are not flaws, but areas that could benefit from some tact and finesse.

9.3. Adapting to the Director

Communicating effectively with a Director requires you to be straightforward and concise. Stick to data, facts, and logic. They appreciate quick, decisive actions and solutions. Patiently accept their criticism, keeping your focus on the goal.

9.4. Adapting to the Expressive

Engage with Expressives by invoking their feelings. Encourage their ideas while subtly steering them towards the topic at hand. Celebrate their victories, support them in their losses, but most importantly, make the communication interactive and enjoyable.

9.5. Adapting to the Thinker

With Thinkers, clearly lay down the process and present data systematically. Be patient and allow time for decisions as they prefer thorough deliberation. Acknowledge their meticulousness, and strive to imbibe some of their structured approach.

9.6. Adapting to the Supportive

To connect with Supportives, create a trust-filled environment and display empathy freely. Listen attentively and validate their feelings. Encourage them to voice their opinions, recognizing their contribution to maintaining harmony.

9.7. Practising Adaptation

Now that the world of communication styles has been unraveled to you, the next step is to practice your adaptations in real-world scenarios. This could range from mindful adapting in everyday conversations, to rehearsing your versatility before major meetings where you expect to encounter diverse styles.

Reflect on the aftermath of every such interaction - what did you do well? What can you improve? Over time, this focused practice will become second nature to you, enabling you to instinctively alter your communication in alignment with your counterpart's style.

Keep in mind that adapting does not mean changing who you are. Rather, it's about expanding your ability to connect with a variety of people in a way that allows mutual understanding and respect to flourish.

9.8. Developing Emotional Intelligence and Empathy

Emotional Intelligence (EI) and empathy play a significant role in successful adaptation. Having a high EI means that you are aware of your own and others' feelings, and can manage them effectively. Empathy takes this a step further; it allows you to feel what others feel, making your adaptation more authentic and compelling.

The development of EI and empathy can be fostered by regularly putting yourself in others' shoes, acknowledging different perspectives, and managing your own emotions responsibly.

9.9. The Versatility Master

As we wrap up this fascinating voyage, recognize that becoming a Versatility Master is a continuous journey of self-improvement. It necessitates patience, practice, and persistence. But above all, it involves turning every interaction into an opportunity to learn, grow, and adapt.

Let this be not a daunting task but a captivating challenge, as you embark upon the endless ocean of communication versatility. Unleash your potential, let go of judgments, and see the beauty in diversity. Your journey to becoming a communication chameleon begins now!

Chapter 10. Negotiation Techniques for Challenging Personalities

Whether you are negotiating a business deal, resolving a conflict, or just wanting to have a productive conversation with someone you find challenging, the right negotiation techniques can help you steer clear of misunderstandings and reach the desired outcome. It's important to handle conversations with such individuals with patience, understanding, and fierce assertiveness, while maintaining respect for their boundaries.

10.1. Understand Your Interlocutor

Understanding the personality and motivations of the person you are negotiating with is a critical first step. Observe emotional reactions and note what triggers them. Listen to their use of language to understand their worldview. Identifying patterns in their behavior helps in anticipating their response and shaping your communication to encourage agreement rather than conflict.

10.2. Express Yourself Clearly

The clearer your message, the less room there is for interpretation and confusion. Be precise with your choice of words to reduce the chance of nullifying your intentions. Use simple, straight-forward language and avoid industry jargon or slang.

10.3. Active Listening

By actively listening, you delve below the surface of mere words, seeking understanding of the other party's feelings and intentions. This validation can help the challenging person feel heard, respected, and likely more cooperative.

10.4. The Power of Pause

A powerful negotiation tool, pausing allows you to absorb information, formulate responses, and gain control over your emotions. A well-placed silent moment can also emphasize a point or encourage the other party to reveal more.

10.5. Set and Maintain Boundaries

You must clearly express your limits and adhere to them. This gives a sense of stability, reduces anxiety, and discourages manipulative behavior.

10.6. Use 'I' Statements

'I' statements are a way of expressing your thoughts or feelings without sounding accusatory. For example, say "I feel unnoticed when my contributions are overlooked" instead of "You never appreciate my contributions."

10.7. Choose the Right Environment

A calm, neutral environment is conducive to productive communications. Details like seating arrangements, lighting and noise levels can influence the success of the negotiation.

10.8. Stay Calm and Composed

Keeping your emotions in check when dealing with a challenging personality is crucial. If emotions are escalating, it may be better to pause or reschedule the conversation.

10.9. Utilize Neutral Third Parties

In high-stakes negotiations where a challenging personality is affecting progress, bringing in a neutral third party can prove helpful. They can ensure fairness, provide fresh perspective, and mediate the discussions.

It goes without saying that skillful negotiation is not a guileful manipulation but a navigation towards a beneficial outcome for all involved. Assertiveness, diplomacy and empathy are your guiding stars in this journey. Cultivating these skills can transform your challenging interactions into enriching and constructive experiences.

10.10. Have a Game Plan

Before heading into a negotiation, study the situation and the other party, defining your expectations and potential barriers. Anticipating the emotions and actions that may arise allows you to prepare your responses.

10.11. Practice Patience

Negotiation is not a race. Rushing often results in poor decisions and missed opportunities. Keep the conversation pace slow and steady, allowing ample time for reflection and response.

10.12. Stay Flexible

Ability to adapt is essentail in any negotiation. Although you come prepared with a game plan, be open to changing your approach based on the other party's reactions.

10.13. Use Questions Effectively

Pose open-ended questions to encourage the other person to express their concerns or wants. Likewise, use clarifying questions to ensure you understand their viewpoints and interests fully.

10.14. Find Win-Win Solutions

Effective negotiations aim for solutions that benefit all parties. When dealing with challenging personalities, highlighting how the resolution can benefit them increases the likelihood of agreement.

By integrating these techniques in your communication repertoire, you will adeptly navigate your way through complicated conversations. The journey will not always be smooth, but each conversation refines your negotiation skills and builds your confidence. Over time, you will find yourself turning even the most difficult interactions into positive engagements.

Chapter 11. Case Studies and Practice Scenarios of Advanced Tactful Communication

Effective communication is the key to both personal and professional success. By understanding different behavioral patterns and learning the right techniques, any conversation, no matter how challenging, can be turned into a constructive interaction. Let's delve into a collection of riveting case studies and practice scenarios that will showcase just how this can be achieved.

11.1. Case Study 1: Coping With Aggression

Andrea, a middle manager in a multinational corporation, often had to deal with James, a senior co-worker known for his aggressive demands. James had a reputation for dressing down anyone who didn't immediately grasp his complicated instructions.

Instead of reacting defensively, Andrea chose to employ empathy and assertive communication. Andrea listened patiently, confirming that she understood James's points before summarizing them back to him. This way, she maintained control of the conversation while showing respect for James's viewpoints. Andrea also requested more clarity when needed, without diminishing the perceived importance of James's needs.

Andrea's approach would eventually have a tempering effect on James's aggressiveness, leading to more constructive conversations. This case study highlights the importance of patience, assertiveness, and a respect for diversity in communication styles when dealing with aggressive personalities.

11.2. Practice Scenarios

Let's now address a few highly engaging and informative practice scenarios that can help you fine-tune your ability to communicate tactfully.

1. Imagine dealing with a co-worker who consistently arrives late for pre-scheduled meetings, wasting everyone's time. How would you discuss this issue with them without triggering defensiveness?

2. Suppose you need to confront a colleague who is missing deadlines, impacting the overall teamwork. How would you approach this conversation?

3. How would you talk to an overbearing manager who consistently overloads you with tasks without considering your existing workload?

Reflecting on these scenarios can help you apply principles of tactful communication to real-life situations.

11.3. Case Study 2: Managing Disruptive Opinions

Laura, a team leader, found herself often at odds with Alex, a team member who tended to oppose her ideas strongly during team meetings. The ensuing arguments often derailed the team's focus.

Laura decided to take a new approach. Taking the time to approach Alex privately, Laura stated her understanding of his desire to contribute positively to the team. She shared that his strong opposition often created confusion, asking Alex to voice his differing opinions privately before meetings.

Alex was appreciative of Laura's respectful and direct conversation. This led to better teamwork, and it also allowed Alex to contribute constructively without disrupting cohesiveness.

In this case, Laura effectively silenced disruptions by allocating a constructive space in the process for disagreements to be heard and discussed.

11.4. Case Study 3: Encouraging Introverted Personalities

As a Team Lead, David noticed that Sara, although a highly capable member of his team, was often overshadowed by extrovert colleagues during brainstorming sessions.

David decided to adapt his communication approach to guarantee that every member had a voice. He started to pause the discussions occasionally to invite explicit input from less vocal team members like Sara. David also initiated one-on-one meetings where Sara could voice her ideas without the pressure of the group.

Soon, Sara's unique perspectives were recognized and the team benefitted from a richer variety of viewpoints.

Through understanding and accommodating different communication styles, David successfully drew out the strengths of a varied team.

These cases studies, alongside the practice scenarios offer an insight into how understanding, plegance, tact, and patience can make the difference in challenging conversations. By noting and adapting your approach accordingly, your conversations will become more effective, leading to improved personal and professional outcomes.

www.ingramcontent.com/pod-product-compliance
Lightning Source LLC
Chambersburg PA
CBHW071035260726
48661CB00007B/3028